Write a Novel that Sells!

The **Best** Aspiring Author's Guide
To Creating a Bestselling Novel
And Making Your Story the **Best** it can be!

By William Bartlett

https://www.williambartlettauthor.com/

HOW TO BECOME A PUBLISHED AUTHOR

Step One: Just write!

Excuses are the cancer that decay our dreams. And fear is what usually causes us to make excuses. Sometimes insecurity, lack of courage, or lack of confidence also causes us to hesitate when it comes to writing, but it all boils down to fear. So, we end up making excuses not to write.

If you're anything like me, you've had a dream of becoming a published author for a long time. That dream has always seemed achievable to us. We have read many books, and sometimes we find ourselves reading a book that makes us think; man, this book is crap! I could totally write this story better.

It wasn't until we started writing our own book that we realized how difficult it truly is. That was the point where we started to respect published authors. There are a lot of factors to take into consideration when writing a full-length story. It is crucially important to educate yourself on the fundamental structure that makes up a story. Every story needs to have a skeleton, because without one, like our bodies, it would collapse. The stronger the skeleton, the more solid the story!

If you're like me, you've already tried googling elements of story structure, but you have yet to find a straight answer. Every answer seems complicated and unclearly explained. This book will correct that issue once and for all!

So, the answer to the question, how do I become a published author, is quite simple. Just write! Yes, it's important to read a lot. Yes, it's important to educate yourself as much as possible, but that doesn't mean you have to wait! The more you write the better you'll be at it. It's as simple as practice makes perfect.

Before you finish your first book, whether you like it or not, you WILL end up writing dozens of drafts. Write, write, write! And eventually your golden idea will hit you if it hasn't already. And then, you'll write many whole books before you'll have a bestseller.

Step Two: A published author is an amateur writer that never gave up.

I admit, I'm poorly paraphrasing a quote by Richard Bach; "A professional writer is an amateur who didn't quit", but according to the man himself, he didn't make it up. In fact, he always thought he was quoting Samuel Johnson, but could never find any proof of that! I won't go so far as to call this new version of the quote my own, but the message it shares is just too important to ignore.

I am a STRONG believer of not giving up on your dreams. I'm also a fan of the phrase; "If at first you don't succeed, try, try again", but I like to change that phrase a little when I share it with my kids. If at first you don't succeed, fix what you're doing wrong and then try again! If you failed, it's obviously because you did something wrong. Look at yourself and at how you're doing things, correct or improve whatever needs it, and try again. If you fail again, then take *another* look at yourself and at how you're doing things, correct or improve whatever needs it, and then try *yet again*.

"The definition of insanity is doing the same thing over and over again and expecting different results." Is another ambigous quote written by Einstein? No one really knows for sure.

My first attempt at writing a novel was such a massive failure that I was advised to stop trying to write novels and to focus the next several years of my life, possibly even decade, on reading - only reading. This wasn't necessarily bad advice. Based on the severity of the manuscript's broken state, it was probably the best advice anyone could give me.

That manuscript showed me that I had no clue on how to write a novel. But I'm stubborn... better said, determined. I had an idea for a book, so I let raw and uncut creativity flow from my mind, through my hand, and into the manuscript. You will hear from many authors that letting the creativity flow is exactly what you should do, and they're right, but that should be done in the *right way.*

So instead of taking the reasonable advice of not writing until I had grown my total record of 'books-read' tenfold, I decided to read ten writing-advice books. After the ten writing-advice books, I listened to a couple audio-books on character arcs, watched so many YouTube videos that I lost count, read dozens upon dozens of articles, including some from www.writersdigest.com and www.helpingwritersbecomeauthors.com (two of my personal favorites), and read several more classic epic fantasy novels (since I was trying to write an adult Fantasy novel).

After I did all that, can you guess what I did next? I *tried again.* Despite the common advice I was receiving from people, I decided to follow my heart instead. I wanted to become a better writer, so I learned how, and I practiced what I learned. Write, write, write!!! Reading is important, but you don't have to read fifty-thousand books to become a published author. You just need to write one perfect book!

Writing is like playing guitar or shooting three-point baskets; the more you do it, (the right way), the better you get at it. But you must constantly stop, check, and revise. Otherwise, you'll only get better at doing it wrong.

Writing the right way is NOT easy and can get frustrating at times, but if you want to make your dream of becoming a published author come true, you can't quit. You can't be afraid of criticism. You can't let re-writes discourage you. You can't get hung up over having to completely scrap a novel and start over fresh with an entirely new story!

But never give up on your dream of becoming a published author. If at first you don't succeed, fix what you're doing wrong and then try again!

CREATE A BESTSELLING IDEA!

Step One: Don't be so hard on yourself!

Don't worry so much about creating the perfect idea at once. You'll discard ideas that come to you because you'll be afraid they will be judged as stupid, lame, unoriginal, or uninteresting. You'll research until your eyes roll out and never find your perfect and original idea. This will be a colossal waste of your time.

All those little not-so-great-ideas are the individual dollars that will eventually grow into a million-dollar idea! Your ideas will evolve. They will merge. They will complicate and then simplify. You must treat every idea and even the pieces of ideas as gems. Save them, remember them, and record them. They are the seeds that will sprout into the dream idea that you'll won't believe came from your own mind!

You are a writer and you *will* become an author. Treat yourself like one, and never sabotage yourself.

Step Two: Be patient and imaginative.

You will never find an idea out there waiting for you in your research. You know why? Because it doesn't exist yet! A bestselling idea is something that you can't find, it's something that will come to you in its own time.

I have had several bestselling ideas that have hit me during the most unexpected moments, like in the shower, trying to fall asleep, while background-watching a Disney movie, or working out. They materialize in this manner because it is always the final piece of several fragments you have been holding on to. So, you must practice *patience* and wait until it comes to you naturally.

You can't force a bestselling idea. In the meantime, you should be open to new experiences! Read! Watch movies! Travel! Try new foods, meet new people, and change up your routine! Try genres you usually avoid in books and movies. I started to read books in genres I don't particularly favor and discovered some real gems.

I recently read "You" and "Hidden Bodies" by Caroline Kepnes and I was blown away by the originality of her story. It is rare to read a novel where the antagonist is the main character and yet the story still flows successfully. She did an amazing job at writing it. That is a bestselling idea at its finest.

Another one that opened my eyes was "The Handmaid's Tale" by Margaret Atwood. A truly complex and original bestselling idea that stimulates the imagination. Excellent read. So, break out of your comfort zone and discover the gems that are available and up for grabs. That is where you will find your inspiration.

Step Three: Lock up your ideas as they arrive!

Save every idea as they sprout into your mind, so you don't forget them. And more importantly, the process of writing them down will help solidify them in your memory. Form the habit of recording every idea you like, despite your fear of it being small or insignificant. There are many ways of recording them. Voice recorder, tablet, notebook, or pen and paper.

There are digital notebook apps you can download onto your phone that will sync up with your google mail account that will save your notes online. I personally keep organized folders on my Microsoft One Drive account where I have a folder dedicated specifically to ideas. If you don't jot down your ideas, chances are, you will forget them, and you need them to evolve into compound ideas.

Your mind will reward you with more ideas after it remembers the previous ones. Remember, ideas can be elusive, especially late at night when you are lying in bed. That's why I believe your best companion is an app that you have downloaded on your phone. Your phone is something you will always have on your person.

HOW TO STRUCTURE YOUR NOVEL

Novel structure consists of three **key** elements:

Theme
Plot
Character arc

When you've decided what you want the general **theme** of your novel to be (the mood that the reader is left with after they finish your novel, sit back, and ponder the story as a whole), this will be the foundation from which you create your protagonist's **character** and the basis of his/her **arc**. Once you've decided your protagonist's personality and **arc**, that will be the foundation from which you create your entire **plot**.

What's funny, is that once you've decided on what your **plot** will be, that is also what creates your **theme**! It's a cycle that feeds itself. K.M. Weiland defines this wonderfully in a simple graphic found in her excellent article:

https://www.helpingwritersbecomeauthors.com/plot-character-and-theme-the-greatest-love-triangle-in-fiction/

So, what does this mean? In my experience, if you come up with one of the three, chances are the other two will soon follow. But you must be consciously aware of the three key elements and **write them down** as they come to you! These key elements must be foremost in your mind as you structure your novel so that you can successfully craft a beautiful story with a deep and meaningful purpose, that will surely be remembered.

Theme

What is theme? I personally love using examples to define story elements. When someone asks you what your favorite book is, you tell them the title. If the book has a great title, they will be intrigued enough to ask you what the book is about. You might answer by explaining the **plot**: It's about the end of the world. Or you might even answer with the **theme**: It's about discovering if you're willing to sacrifice a few good people for the greater good of mankind. Or you might explain the **characters**: It's about a feisty little girl who ends up saving the world. See the differences there? See the similarities? **Theme** is the lesson learned, the moral of the story, the thoughts you're left with afterwards, the message you want to deliver to the world. To put it simply, **theme** is in the subtext. The message that is being picked up by the reader without it being delivered to them directly. Subtext. Can you guess the theme in the movie "Avatar"? No character or narrator ever spoke the words: It is wrong to invade another's land and harvest it for your own purpose and kill them in the process. But this message was flashing in neon through your mind throughout the entire movie. Why? Theme.

Choosing a theme is easy. What message would you like your story to deliver to its readers? What message would you like to represent as an author? What is an issue or topic that is important to you, that you want to enlighten or remind the world of? Theme is powerful. It is one third of every great story. Without a powerful theme, your story will fall flat like a tripod missing a leg.

Plot

What is plot? Some authors will swear up and down that story structure isn't needed! That writing is an art and that a good author can write without structuring their story at all and it organically creates its own cohesive flow.

Liars!

Then why is it that the stories written by these talented authors who don't need structure, always come out with perfectly placed plot points, plot twists with appropriate foreshadowing in all the right places, and with a climax so properly built up with tension it has you biting your fingernails? Because the author structured it!

I do believe it is possible to read enough novels to where your subconscious becomes so familiar with structure that it becomes second nature when writing your own story, that everything falls into place naturally. That is definitely possible. But it is rare and unrealistic. Besides, ain't nobody got time for that! It is always better to play it safe and structure your novel ahead of time to avoid too many rewrites.

This plot structure is based on the Three-Act Story. Percentages are based off an 80,000-word novel.

ACT ONE

The Hook! - 1% mark

This is the opening moment of your story *and* your opening scene! This is the first thing that happens in your story – probably even the first line. The hook is what will capture the reader's attention and pique their interest in your story. Sometimes the very first word will pique enough interest to lead them to read the rest of the sentence.

A good first sentence will lead the reader to finishing the paragraph. By then their interest will turn into intrigue, and they will want to finish the page! By then, they will really want to know how this specific event will end and they might even finish the chapter. Here is an example: Every time I die, I learn something new about the real world.

This sentence raises new questions and creates intrigue. This single plot event can make the difference between a reader continuing or placing the book back on the shelf. It is <u>crucial</u>!

In-between Meat - 1%-12%
All the chapter from the hook to the Inciting event will serve the purpose of building up tension, getting to know the characters, and especially the normal world before it gets shattered by the inciting incident.

The Inciting Event! - 12% mark
This is the BIG moment that will change the protagonist's world forever! Something big will happen. This is a turning point that takes place halfway through the First Act. This is the Call to Adventure; the moment the protagonist's Normal World is significantly affected by the main story's conflict.

The Build Up - 12% - 25%
The final pieces necessary for the main conflict to be set in motion are moved into position, while ramping up the tension and <u>revealing the stakes</u>.

First Plot Point/Key Event - 25% mark
This transition point in your story is the gateway between the end of the First Act and the beginning of the Second. Also, this is a great place to put the Key Event. Syd Field's excellent book: "Screenplay" explains: "The Inciting incident… sets the story in motion… [while] the key incident [is] what the story is about and draws the main character into the story line."
The Inciting Event and the Key Event are two different things but

are often placed in the same spot. The Key Event is the point when the character can't avoid getting involved with the story's main conflict any longer because of the Inciting Event rocking his/her world. This is where it gets personal for the protagonist.

ACT TWO

Reaction - 25% - 37%

After the First Plot Point, your main character struggles a bit to understand the obstacles thrown in his way by the antagonist.

The First Pinch Point! - 37% mark

This is a big setback for the protagonist. This section will serve as a reminder of the antagonist's power, which reveals new clues about the origin of the main conflict.

Realization - 37% - 50%

The protagonist's realization grows, and his/her reactions become more informed.

The Midpoint! - 50% mark

This is where you put your <u>Moment of Truth</u>! It is when the protagonist realizes the whole truth about the nature of the main conflict. All your planned shocking truths are revealed here! Reader finds out here WHY everything is happening.

Action - 50% - 62%

Now that the protagonist is blessed with knowledge, he/she finally gains some success against the antagonist.

The Second Pinch Point! - 62% mark

Another big setback for the protagonist. This section will foreshadow the Third Plot Point and serves to remind the protagonist what is at stake if he/she fails!

Renewed Push - 62% - 75%
Protagonist fights back! And he/she gains a decent victory, or so it seems...

ACT THREE

The Third Plot Point! - 75% mark
The decent victory is <u>shattered</u> by a HUGE set back/pinch point. This one hurts.

Recovery 75% - 88%
Protagonist is set back big time and hesitates. He/she doubts themselves and begins to question his/her choices, his/her commitment to their goal, and his/her own worth and ability. Doubt consumes your protagonist.

The Climax!!! - 88% mark
Something will happen here that is a turning point in the plot and forces the protagonist and the antagonist to finally and unavoidably face each other.

The Confrontation! - 88% - 98%
This is the final battle, final fight, final championship game, final confrontation, etc. This is the duel to the death, literally or metaphorically. What happens here will mean the protagonist and antagonist cannot both walk away.

The Climactic Moment! - 98% mark
This is moment the protagonist finally accomplishes his/her goal! It now becomes a physical impossibility for the main conflict to continue. It's over!

The Resolution - 98% - 100%

Now you will ease the reader out of the excitement of the Climax and into the final emotion of your story. Wrap it up and tie off loose ends! If you want to leave a loose end that leads into a sequel, then create <u>only one</u>!

Character arc

What is a character arc? It is not enough to just write a great character. You gotta right a character that goes through an emotional journey that the reader can resonate with! The best stories have a character that is changed by the events of the plot.

One of my favorite character arcs is from a movie: Anakin Skywalker from the Star Wars Saga. This is one of the most well-known Negative Change Arcs. You follow along as the story's plot affects him as a boy, teenager, and young adult. We watch him lose control of his emotions as he slowly becomes corrupted by the dark side.

He begins his journey as an innocent well-intentioned kid, full of hope and positive energy. There is even a prophecy revolving around the character, that he is the promised one, immaculately concepted by the force itself, destined to bring balance to the force.

We watch him make bad choices, albeit small ones, but several that work in chain reaction that ultimately leaves him lost and blind in the depths of the dark side. He instead becomes one of the most powerful and most difficult villains to defeat in the history of the universe!

What made this journey so emotional to us was how cleverly written his character arc was. This is the power that a character arc can have in a story. This is how we know that character arcs are as equally important as the plot itself!

In her book Creating Character Arcs, K.M. Weiland says: "Plot and character are integral to one another, plot structure and character arc are integral to one another." In his guide: Story, Robert McCee says: "We cannot ask which is more important, structure or character, because structure is character; character is structure. They're the same thing, and therefore one cannot be more important than the other."

The protagonist's arc *is* the emotion of the story. This allows for a *theme* to be present. These key elements are what will make your story memorable!

There are five foundational elements that must be decided about your protagonist before you begin structuring your novel. Your protagonist must have:

1. A major story <u>GOAL</u>
2. A <u>LIE</u> that he/she believes
3. Something that he/she <u>WANTS</u>
4. Something that he/she <u>NEEDS</u>
5. A <u>GHOST</u>

<u>The five foundational elements</u>:

Your character's major story goal:

Your character and reader usually discover this after the inciting event takes place (the event that takes place in your story that changes everything in your protagonist's life). This when your character has a fairly good idea of what he/she must do. This is usually what needs to happen to complete the plot at the end of the story.

Example: Billy needs to stop the evil queen from killing every man in the world. Stop her from obtaining the amulet of strength or she will become impossible to stop.

The lie your character believes:

This is your character's inner weakness. It is something they believe to be true because it has worked well for them thus far... until now (the inciting event).

Example: Billy believes he is too small and weak to defeat the evil queen.

The thing your character wants:

Keep in mind the thing your character wants is different from his major story goal. Your character will have small goals, like from scene to scene, and major story goals. These are plot related and not the same as want your character wants. The thing your character wants comes from something deep. Something they think will cure their feelings inside. These feelings usually come from your character's ghost. The thing they want is usually something physical, something external, that will make everything better. Your character might be depressed(feelings) because her boyfriend broke up with her (ghost), and wants that new promotion, to make more money, to by new things. Only then will her life feel better(wants).

Example: Billy wants to find the amulet of strength to keep it from the evil queen, but also to use its powers himself, to become strong (enough to defeat the evil queen)

The thing your character needs:

To put it simply, the thing your character needs is to realize the **truth**. Your protagonist has been blinded by this lie they believe throughout the entire story. The sequence of the plot is what reveals to your protagonist clue by subtle clue, what the truth really is and why the lie they believe has been holding them back all along. Close to the end of the story, your protagonist will finally embrace the truth they **need**, and it will set them free, and preferably will be what they needed to finally defeat the antagonist.

Example: Billy finally realizes he never needed strength or power to defeat the evil queen. All he needed was courage and to use his intelligence.

Your character's ghost:

Your protagonist's ghost is something that haunts them. Something the happened in their past prevents them from seeing truths clearly. It messed up the way the see the world and has left them with a **lie** that they believe.

Example: Billy's mother was murdered by horse thieves when he was a young boy. He was young, weak, powerless, and scared to stop them and save her.

After creating these five foundational characteristics, the rest of your character arc planning will come together naturally!

THE THREE CHARACTER ARC TYPES

1. POSITIVE CHANGE ARC
2. FLAT ARC
3. NEGATIVE CHANGE ARC

Positive Change Arc:

The positive change arc is probably the most common arc used in stories. Why? Mostly because people like happy endings. But the thing that makes a happy ending so satisfying is the delivery of what you've subconsciously wanted to happen all along. How did you even know what you wanted to see at the end of the story? You were manipulated by a well-structured and cohesive plot, character arc, and theme.

The positive change arc consists of three basic parts:
I. Your protagonist believes the **lie.**
II. Your protagonist overcomes the **lie.**
III. The new learned **truth** will set your protagonist free.

If you skipped the five foundational characteristics of your protagonist, now's the time to go back and do it! You will need them now as we create the skeleton of your arc. This is the order you want to put the trail of subtle clues that will manipulate your reader's subconscious in the direction you want them to think:

Act one (1% - 25% of your story)

1% Believes lie

At the very beginning of your story, your main character will believe a lie that has worked for him/her so far in their current "normal world" (this is what is life is like before the inciting event changes their life forever).

Example: Billy believes he is too small to defeat anyone bigger or stronger than him in combat, because he never has. And this has kept him safe.

12% First hint lie will no longer work.

This is right around your inciting event, the part in plot where something happens that will change your protagonist's world forever. Something else will happen, that is hopefully related somehow, that will show the protagonist that maybe – just maybe – the **lie** is is actually a lie and not the truth, as the character currently believes. This is the **truth** peeking through the plot as a hint, that maybe the **lie** isn't always the case.

Example: The evil Queen conquers Billy's village easily and enslaves some of the people. But during the battle, he witnesses a smaller person like himself outsmart one of the Queen's guards by using a trap. The small person then evades the trapped attacker. This reminds him of a plan he and his peers would use to trap big game when hunting, big and dangerous game that could easily kill them if they failed to execute the plan with precision.

25% Lie no longer effective.

This will happen around your first plot point. Something else happens (because of the first plot point) that really opens your character's eyes to the **lie** being a lie and not the truth. Because of the plot moving forward, this first plot point puts your protagonist in a position where they are forced to let go of the lie, they still believe, even for a moment.

Example: After enslaved and sent to a slave camp where everyone is assigned a duty station and then split up and sent out, Billy and his friends/family realize they must act now and escape, or they will never see each other again. Even though Billy still believes he is powerless against the big and strong enslavers, he knows that if he does nothing, he and his family/friends will suffer greatly.

Act Two (25% to 75% of your story)

37% Punished for using Lie.

Now we are in the second act of your story. At this point your character will try to hold on to the lie when he really should have tried the truth. He will be punished for this erroneous choice. This mistake is also the cause of the first pinch point in the plot.

Example: Billy fails in his part of the escape plan because he doubts his ability to perform successfully against a mighty enslaver once he sees him.

50% Moment of Truth: Sees Truth (but doesn't reject Lie)

This is a major turning point for the character as well as the plot itself. Your character finds himself in a situation where they realize that they must absolutely try the **truth** in order for the plot to move forward. They can see the **truth** clearly now and know what they must do. This is an eye-opening moment for your protagonist.

Example: The evil queen sets up an ambush and attacks the group by surprise. Everyone is subdued but Billy was able to evade capture. He realizes he is the only one who can free the rest of his group and if he does not act, they will all be executed. He clings to the **lie** out of fear and doubt, clearly sees the **truth,** and knows what he must do.

62% Rewarded for effectively using Truth.

This is will typically happen as a reaction to the second pinch point. Your character will use the truth and he will be rewarded by it. The following is a singular example, but keep in mind, from this point on, your protagonist will be using the truth more and more with small actions that will bring him closer and closer to achieving his ultimate plot goal. He will be rewarded each time by his/her successes.

Example: After Billy launches his plan to free everyone, they are left scrambling in a fight against the guards. Billy finds himself in a situation where he must save one of his companion's life. His companion is fighting for their life and is losing. The only way Billy can save his life is the exact same way he could have saved his mother's life when he was young. The situation resembles the one from his childhood when he was too afraid to act so much that his fears and doubt have elevated to a maximum level. Here he is forced to choose. He must be brave, face his fear, overcome his doubts, and act to save the life of his companion (**truth**, because he is capable), or flee and save his own life because he knows he isn't capable of saving anyone and will only get them both killed (**lie**). He musters up the courage needed and attacks the threat to his companion, distracting him long enough for his companion to slip free. They execute the rest of the plan previously set together and kill the attacker, turn the rest of the battle towards their favor (**reward**).

Act Three (75%-100% of your story)

75% Rejects Lie

At this point something awful will happen in the plot that really influences the protagonist's **lie** and **truth** dilemma. After the second pinch point, everything was looking good for your protagonist. He/she had reached a bit of a victory. But your character hasn't fully let go of the **lie** yet, they only saw how the **truth** worked for that specific situation. This is your third plot point. This is the most important moment for your character's arc. Here, the antagonist bounces back and puts your character in a real tough spot. This is where your character will feel completely defeated but will fully reject the **lie**. Now, your character will fully embrace the truth, they will see what is at stake and what they stand to lose if they don't get their act together.

Example: The Evil Queen finally gets her hands on the amulet and uses its power to become monstrously strong. Billy feels defeated as his doubts tell him the evil queen will be impossible to defeat now. She has the extra strength and he has none. He knows now, that he will have to find a way to defeat her as he is, little and weak, or else she will surely accomplish her goal of conquering all the land and enslaving every last man alive.

88% Embraces Truth.

This is your climax in the plot. This is the final showdown between your protagonist and the antagonist. This is the moment where your protagonist will either get the thing they **want** or not, or they might have to sacrifice it completely for the greater good. At this point your character also knows that the **lie** is not the way to go and by only using **truth** will he/she be victorious. No doubt about it.

Example: The evil queen has all of Billy's companions captured. Billy is truly on his own and must defeat the queen on his own. He puts all of his trust in an old plan he and his peers would use to trap big game when hunting, big and dangerous game that could easily kill him if he failed to execute the plan with precision. He trusts the plan because he is confident in the truth now. He knows that despite his size it is still possible to defeat any foe. He executes the plan flawlessly and defeats the queen.

98% Uses Truth to gain Need.

The protagonist has finally defeated the antagonist or has ended the antagonistic threat. He/she gains the thing he/she **needs** because of everything he/she has learned from the **truth**. This is also the moment where your character could gain the thing they **want** or possibly have to sacrifice it in light of gaining the thing they **need** (the truth).

Example: Billy stands over the queen's corpse and sees the amulet of strength around her neck. He rips it off and looks at it as he ponders everything he has learned. He considers for a moment taking the amulet for himself. It is the thing he always wanted. He places it on a rock. Then he smashes it pieces. The glow of its power fades into nothing.

100% Enters new Truth-Empowered Normal World.

The world has now returned to its normal state or has become a new normal world, but the protagonist is forever changed in a positive way, because of the events of this positive change arc! Example: Billy frees his companions and they return home to their original village. Billy teaches the youth of the village how anyone can be a hero, regardless of their size, gender, culture, or age.

<u>Later I will show you how to intertwine this with your plot structure so you may outline your novel perfectly</u>.

The Flat Arc:

The flat arc is probably the second most popular character arc found in novels, movies, and stories in general. In a positive change arc, the changing world affects the protagonist throughout and forces him/her to change in a positive way. The events of the plot cause a change inside the protagonist. In a flat arc, the protagonist doesn't change inside, although sometimes the plot will change him/her externally, but nothing inside. In this story, the protagonist is the one changing the world and characters around him/her. The events of the plot will test the protagonist throughout the entire story and challenge his/her morals, values, and convictions. The protagonist will be tempted to let go of the **truth** they already believe or even cause doubt, but ultimately the protagonist's belief in the truth will never be changed.

The positive change arc consists of three basic parts:
I.   Your protagonist already believes the **truth.**
II.   Your protagonist maintains belief in the **truth**, although he/she is tested.
III.   Your protagonist uses the truth to overcome the world's **lie**.

If you skipped the five foundational characteristics of your protagonist, now's the time to go back and do it! You will need them now as we create the skeleton of your arc. This is the order you want to put the trail of subtle clues that will manipulate your reader's subconscious in the direction you want them to think:

Act One (1%-25%)

1% Believes Truth in a Lie-Ridden World

The protagonist believes a Truth that the rest of the Normal World around her rejects. The Normal World and most of its characters are mired in a central Lie which enslaves them in some way.

12% Challenged to Use Truth to Oppose Lie

The Call to Adventure, when the protagonist first encounters the main conflict, presents a direct challenge to her Truth. The question at this point is whether or not she can be convinced to take action in wielding her Truth against the Lie of the world around her.

25% World Tries to Forcibly Impose Lie

The protagonist is faced with a consequential choice, in which the antagonistic force attempts to forcibly impose the Lie upon her or others. In refusing to relinquish her Truth for the Lie, the protagonist passes through a Door of No Return, in which she is forced to leave the Normal World of the First Act and enter the Adventure World of the main conflict in the Second Act.

Act Two (25%-75%)

37% Uncertain if Truth Is Capable of Defeating Lie

The protagonist struggles to use her Truth against the strength of the antagonistic force's Lie. She doubts whether her Truth can defeat the Lie and, as a result, if it is indeed the Truth.

50% Proves Power of Truth to World

The protagonist perseveres in following her Truth. She offers a Moment of Truth to the world around her. This is the first time the protagonist will demonstrably exhibit the full power and purity of the Truth. At least one significant supporting character will be impacted (positively or negatively) by this revelation.

62%: The Second Pinch Point: Lie-Driven Characters Fight Back

In response to the protagonist's powerful demonstration of Truth at the Midpoint, other Lie-driven characters will double down on the Lie and use it to mount a formidable counterattack upon the protagonist and her Truth.

Act Three (75%-100%)

75% Lie Seems to Triumph Externally

The Lie-driven tactics of the antagonistic force hit the protagonist hard, even to the point of the protagonist's seeming defeat in the external conflict. The protagonist is confronted by a "low moment" brought about by the supporting characters' continuing refusal to fully reject the Lie. The protagonist must confront the true stakes of what she stands to sacrifice if she continues to embrace the Truth. Even in the face of overwhelming odds, she reaffirms her conviction of the Truth.

88% Final Confrontation Between Truth and Lie

The protagonist enters the final confrontation with the antagonistic force to decide whether or not she will gain the Thing She Wants. She consciously and explicitly embraces and wields the Truth.

98% Truth Defeats Lie

The protagonist uses the Truth (often with the help of positively-changed supporting characters) to defeat the antagonistic force and gain the Thing She Wants and Needs (which are often the same thing in a Flat Arc, since the protagonist always possesses an understanding of the Truth).

100% New Truth-Empowered Normal World

The protagonist enters a new Normal World, which is empowered by the Truth thanks to her actions.

Negative Change Arc:

The negative change arc can happen in a few different ways. Here I will go over the most used one: The Corruption Arc. For an excellent read that elaborates on the subject, please see Creating Character Arcs by K.M. Weiland. The Corruption Arc is basically a story where the character starts out in a world that already knows and embraces the **truth**. He/she has every opportunity to do the same but is lured away by the **lie**. Just as the seed of the **truth** is already latent in the life of a positive change arc character, the seed of the **lie** is latent in the corruption-arc character—even though the **truth** is already right in front of him. This is perhaps the most moving of all the arcs, since it features a character who is good—or at least has a potential for greatness but throws it all away and consciously chooses darkness. Perfect example is the corruption of Anakin Skywalker.

The corruption arc consists of three basic parts:

I. Your protagonist can see the **truth.**
II. Your protagonist rejects the **truth.**
III. Your protagonist embraces the **lie.**

If you skipped the five foundational characteristics of your protagonist, now's the time to go back and do it! You will need them now as we create the skeleton of your arc. This is the order you want to put the trail of subtle clues that will manipulate your reader's subconscious in the direction you want them to think:

Act One (1%-25%)

1% Understands Truth

The protagonist lives in a Normal World that allows for or even encourages the thematic Truth. As a result, the protagonist starts out with an understanding of the Truth.

12% First Temptation of Lie

The Call to Adventure, when the protagonist first encounters the main conflict, also brings the first subtle temptation that the Lie might be able to serve the protagonist *better* than the Truth.

25% Enters Beguiling Adventure World of Lie

The protagonist is faced with a consequential choice, in which he is enticed out of the First Act's safe, Truth-based Normal World into the Second Act's beguiling, Lie-based Adventure World. Not realizing the danger (or believing he is weighing the consequences), the protagonist is lured through the Door of No Return by the promise of the Thing He Wants.

Act Two (25%-75%)

37% Torn Between Truth and Lie

The protagonist is torn between his old Truth and the new Lie. The Lie proves itself effective in moving him nearer the Thing He Wants. But he wages an internal conflict as he recognizes he is moving further and further away from his old convictions and understandings of the world.

50% Embraces Lie Without Fully Rejecting Truth

The protagonist encounters a Moment of Truth in which he comes face to face with the Lie in all its power. He recognizes he cannot gain the Thing He Wants *without* the Lie. Although he is not yet willing to reject the Truth fully and consciously, he makes the decision to fully embrace the Lie.

62% Resists Sacrifice Demanded by Truth

The protagonist is "rewarded" for using the Lie. Building upon what he learned at the Midpoint, the protagonist will start implementing Lie-based actions in combating the antagonistic force and reaching toward the Thing He Wants. The Truth pulls on him, demanding sacrifices he is not willing to give. He begins resisting the Truth more and more adamantly.

Act Three (75%-100%)

75% Embraces Lie

The protagonist utterly rejects the Truth and embraces the Lie. He acts upon this in a way that creates a "low moment" for the world around him (and for him morally, even if he refuses to recognize it). He is now willing to knowingly endure the consequences of rejecting the Truth in exchange for what he sees as the rewards of embracing the Lie.

88% Final Push to Gain Want

The protagonist enters the final confrontation with the antagonistic force to decide whether or not he will gain the Thing He Wants. Unhampered by the Truth, he pushes forward ruthlessly toward his plot goal.

98% Moral Failure

The protagonist uses the Lie and all it has taught him in an attempt to gain the Thing He Wants. He may gain the Thing He Wants and remain senseless to the evil engendered by his actions. Or he may gain the Thing He Wants only to be devastated when he realizes it wasn't worth what he sacrificed. Or he may fail to gain the Thing He Wants and be devastated by the realization that his sacrifices to the Lie were fruitless. One way or another, he definitively ends the conflict between himself and the antagonistic force.

100% Aftermath

The protagonist must confront the aftermath of his choices. He may turn away from the Lie, admitting his mistake and accepting the consequences. Or he may callously forge ahead, intent on continuing to use the Lie to further his own ends.

WHY YOUR NOVEL STILL NEEDS HELP

There are **four** extremely important factors that amateurs are ignorant of. Not anymore. Here are the not-so-secret <u>secrets</u> that will make your Novel different and memorable.

The secret factors:

PROSE

SHOWING NOT TELLING

SCENE STRUCTURE

FORESHADOWING

PROSE

Prose is what makes authors artists and our stories art. Prose is the talent that makes authors stand apart from writers. If story structure is the subject and pre-chosen colors for the painting, and the outline is the sketch of the painting, then **prose** is the beauty of the actual brush strokes. If your brush strokes are not broad in the proper places and soft where they need to be, the painting will not be aesthetically pleasing. Without proper prose, your story will not have the desired effect on its reader.

This, in my opinion, is the *toughest* part of becoming an author. It is not something that can be learned how to do by simply reading about it. It is learned through practice. This is exactly why the most common advice you'll hear from published authors is to read, read, read, and write, write, write. Writing is a skill that is learned through repetition. And your prose is something that will never stop improving.

Remember: Writing is lifting the weight, and reading is your personal trainer; guiding you and making sure you're keeping good form as well as keeping you motivated.

Prose is the way you write your story. There is a big difference between storytelling and story writing. I am an excellent storyteller, but I've had to work awfully hard at turning that skill into story writing. Becoming an author is becoming a master of wordcraft. That means mastering the following elements:

Grammar
Voice
Description
Dialogue
Pacing
POV
Word choice

(Checkout
https://www.helpingwritersbecomeauthors.com/a-writer-or-a-storyteller/ for and excellent explanation of this.)

Writing a story with beautiful prose means using a better vocabulary that we usually speak with, but not pretentious that your story becomes a literary novel, unless you are in fact writing one. You want your prose to flow smoothly as it is read and not the type of writing that causes your reader to lean in close and re-read the sentence slowly to comprehend what you are trying to explain. Good prose is a book that can be read with such a good flow that it's almost being skimmed.

SHOWING NOT TELLING

Took me a couple of years to understand what people meant by this and I couldn't seem to find a helpful explanation. Showing instead of telling as you write your story is the difference between storytelling and story writing.

When you tell your reader what is happening, you are boring them. When you show them what is happening, you are putting them inside the story so they can experience it first-hand.

Telling:
Jane feels sad when she kills her opponent.

Showing a little better, but still telling:
Jane is stricken with remorse as she presses her sword into her opponent's chest.

Showing:
Spraying blood wets her already teared face when she yanks her sword free from her opponent's chest.

Telling summarizes in a bear-minimum type of way. Showing helps the reader experience the details alongside the character. Don't state that a character feels sad, describe what happens when someone feels sad, tears well up, vison blurs, heart races, lips tighten, breath shortens, etc.

Practice this as you write, and your prose will improve with it.

Here's a couple of tips that'll help:

- Don't stress over showing rather than telling every single action throughout the entire novel, or you'll risk making them all less interesting. Save your best showing sentences for the interesting actions of your scenes. Less important actions don't need to be as dramatized.

- Avoid "telling" verbs:

Saw
Smelled
Heard
Felt

And instead write what it is that the character is: seeing/smelling/hearing/feeling.

Becoming a successful author is largely dependent on learning how to appropriately show and tell. If you can master the skill of artfully showing the most important scenes to your readers, then you're already halfway there!

SCENE STRUCTURE

Here is another secret of good writing that most people don't realize is necessary. Again, these three secrets will become a subconscious flow as you write, but only after reading thousands of books. That is why reading is so important. And practicing your craft consistently. Scene structure gives your chapters direction. When your chapters are directionless, they feel unimportant and readers are more likely to put the book down due to confusion and loss of interest. Structuring your scenes is quite simple once you wrap your head around it.

*Note: Multiple scenes can be in one chapter, but you should definitely have at least one full scene in a chapter. I personally like to make every chapter its own scene, but sometimes my Reaction scenes are short enough to throw in with the Action scene.

There are two types of scenes:
Action Scene
Reaction Scene

THE ACTION SCENE:
The action scene is your most common scene and you'll probably have more of these then reaction scenes. The action scene tends to be the more exciting scene hence the name.

Goal:
The scene starts with the protagonist's short term and immediate goal and should be something that will move the protagonist or the plot forward towards the bigger overall goal.
Simple example: Billy's overall story goal is to escape the dungeon he is in, but the short term and immediate goal of this scene is to escape his cell.
Complex example: Billy needs to escape his dungeon cell quickly because today is his execution day.

Conflict:
Halfway through this scene the protagonist will face a conflict that will throw a wrench into the works. This will force the pro-

tagonist to make a new plan, on the spot, to overcome the conflict that is preventing him from accomplishing his goal.

Simple example: The cell is locked.

Complex example: Billy has a key delivered to him and he unlocks the door but when he steps out into the hallway, he finds the guard and the executioner waiting for him.

Disaster:

This is the result of the conflict and will lead the story right into the next scene.

Here, you can choose whether the protagonist achieves his/her goal, doesn't really matter, but there still needs to be a disaster. Here are two examples, one where the disaster is the fact that the protagonist failed in achieving the goal as a result of the conflict, and the other where the protagonist achieves the goal but there is still a disaster that resulted from the conflict. I personally believe the second type of disaster should be the end of as many action scenes as possible as it makes for a more dynamic story.

Simple example one: A previously bribed guard comes through and delivers him a key. The key breaks inside the lock. New goal: find another way out.

Simple example two: The key works and he gets out, but now the guard wants another bribe.

Complex example one: Billy gets locked up again. New goal: find another way out.

Complex example two: Billy must fight the guard and the executioner at the same time. He accidentally kills the guard but the executioner escapes. Now, Billy is injured, and the executioner will likely sound the alarm giving him even less time, higher stakes, and increases the tension.

This well executed action scene naturally flows us right into the reaction scene:

THE REACTION SCENE:

The reaction scene tends to be less exciting as its purpose is to portray the protagonist's reactions to the event that just took place in the action scene but is essential for emotion and theme.

These are the scenes where the protagonist personally reacts to what just happened! This is the reader's chance to experience emotion alongside the protagonist. This is the scene where the reader connects and bonds with the protagonist. The following examples will be based off the **Disaster two** examples.

Reaction:
This section is the juice of the fruit. The importance of sharing the protagonist's emotions with the reader is paramount. These are the moments that make your characters real and relatable. This section you'll show your character's reaction to what just happened in the action scene and the disaster. Sometimes the reaction will be a short and simple one, no more than a gasp, and then lead right into the **decision**. Sometimes it'll be streaming tears, a full-on nervous breakdown, or even a heart attack.

Simple example two: Now that the guard wants another bribe, the reaction here will be surprise and feelings of betrayal. You'll have to flex your newfound showing and not telling skills to properly portray the emotions.

Complex example two: The reaction here is complicated and makes for an excellent scene. Billy's knee is turned sideways, and blood is streaming out of his thigh and it's not stopping. Pain is burning him. He's fatigued. Panic rises in his chest and threatens to overwhelm him.

Dilemma:
Now your protagonist faces a dilemma. They must figure out what to do next. How they can undo the disaster or how to escape it. The disaster placed a major obstacle in the way and the dilemma is your protagonist figuring out how to overcome it. Most of the time, this part of the reaction scene will be obvious through the subtext.

Simple example two: Billy has only moments to realize the dilemma. He realizes the guard betrayed him for selfish reasons and is greedy. The guard knows Billy has nothing else to offer as bribe and has no plans of letting him escape. Billy realizes two options, promise him riches after he escapes, or fight his way out now that he is out of the cell.

Complex example two: Billy's dilemma is time. More guards will soon be barreling down the hallway. He realizes that they will kill him on sight now and he needs to make his escape while injured and bleeding.

Decision:

Now your protagonist must make a decision. Based on the pace of your story, they might spend some time regrouping, open up some maps and plan, sit in their cell and ponder, or make an on the spot decision and keep going. Either way, this is the answer to the dilemma they just realized. They will decide what action to take, which will set them up for the next action scene, in which they will execute the decision made here.

Simple example two: Billy realizes that his diplomatic approach has been getting him nowhere, so he decides to fight the guard.

Complex example two: Billy remembers a previously foreshadowed healer that was willing to help him if he ever needed it. He decides to find him to stop the bleeding first, then he'll make a new plan along the way.

The style of "winging-it" and "plan-as-you-go" writing found in my **complex examples**, forces the story to be more cause-and-effect based, which makes for a much more exciting story. This also helps the reader feel tension and suspense alongside the protagonist who also doesn't know what might happen next. That also helps the reader bond with your protagonist as they will subconsciously root for their success.

If you loosely follow these guidelines as you write your chapters, it will launch your writing skill into the stratosphere. This structure is not something that necessarily needs to be followed perfectly, but definitely needs to be present in your subconscious as you write. Just like showing versus telling, this is something that will be come second nature the more you practice writing, and you be grow progressively better at it.

FORESHADOWING

Foreshadowing is pretty simple and easy to understand. It is even easier to implement in your writing. But it is EXTREMELY important to do, without fail. Ever. You can never, ever, forget to foreshadow the important things.

Foreshadowing consists of two parts:
The Setup
The Payoff

The cliché "woman being chased by a killer into a car that doesn't start" is easily fixed by showing in an earlier chapter that her car was having engine problems. A couple of scenes where she is reminded to add more oil to the car, but the events of the plot keep distracting her and so she forgets, makes the intense car not starting scene, so much more valid. (Don't ever add this scene, foreshadowed or not, into your story, ever, please.)

If Billy is fighting the Vampire King at the climax of your story and he just can't seem to beat his superior strength and agility, then he will need the help of something else. He grabs the silver sword of a thousand truths off the wall and finally kills the Vampire King. Big deal. Not really satisfying. But if the fact that silver is poison to vampires was previously shown, that would make it more interesting. If the silver sword of a thousand truths was shown and maybe even briefly talked about early in the story, that would also make the climax more satisfying. If the very room they are fighting in was shown in the very beginning of the novel, and you carefully planned all the events of the plot to lead Billy far from it and eventually back to it, that will create a sense of completion and closure. All these elements work together to make a truly satisfying climax. Foreshadowing is what made it all possible.

Keep in mind, the payoff is not limited to the climax. <u>The answer to any dilemma</u> that your protagonist faces needs to be foreshadowed.

BEST WISHES

Becoming a successful author is difficult to say the least. Remember: If it were easy, everybody would be rich. Balancing all the elements necessary for a best-selling story is learned skill through practice and many failures. But don't give up. You'll make it if you keep at it.

I'll leave you with an outline template that I use. It has the elements of plot and character arc organized for you, to keep your writing on track. I hope this guide was helpful.

Note
The most valuable elements I used here was taken directly from Katie Weiland's: https://www.helpingwritersbecomeauthors.com/

My goal in publishing this guide was to combine all the necessary elements of a bestselling novel in an easy to read and easy to understand format. Please visit my webpage if interested in my editing services at:
https://www.williambartlettauthor.com/

OUTLINE TEMPLATE

THEME:
[Write your intended theme here]

CHARACTER ARC INFORMATION:
The Positive Change Arc:
Character believes LIE>
Overcomes LIE>
New TRUTH is liberating

Character's major story GOAL:
[Write info here]

The LIE your character believes:
[Write info here]

The TRUTH that your character will learn:
[Write info here]

The Thing your character WANTS:
[Write info here]

The Thing your character NEEDS:
[Write info here]

Your character's GHOST:
[Write info here]

Characteristic Moment:
[Write info here]

The Normal World:
[Write info here]

STORY STRUCTURE

Black text means Plot info.
Red text means Character Arc info.
Blue text means your info.

ACT ONE

PROLOGUE 0% mark
[Optional]

HOOK 1% mark
This opening moment is your opening scene – the first thing that happens in your story – possibly even the first line.
1% The Hook: Believes Lie
The protagonist believes a Lie that has so far proven necessary or functional in the existing Normal World.
[Write info here]

(set-up) 1%-12%
Readers learn about your characters, their goals, and the stakes.
[Write info here]

INCITING EVENT 12% mark
A turning point occurs halfway through the First Act. This is the Call to Adventure, the moment the Normal World is significantly rocked by the conflict.
12% The Inciting Event: First Hint Lie Will No Longer Work
The Call to Adventure, when the protagonist first encounters the main conflict, also brings the first subtle hint that the Lie will no longer serve the protagonist as effectively as it has in the past.
[Write info here]

(build-up) 12% - 25%
The final pieces necessary for the main conflict are moved into position, while ramping up the tension.
[Write info here]

FIRST PLOT POINT 25% mark
The doorway between the end of the First Act and the beginning of the Second. Also, likely to be the Key Event.
25% The First Plot Point: Lie No Longer Effective
The protagonist is faced with a consequential choice, in which

the "old ways" of the Lie-ridden First Act show themselves ineffective in the face of the main conflict's new stakes. Although the protagonist does not yet recognize the inefficacy of the Lie, he will still pass through a Door of No Return, in which he is forced to leave the Normal World of the First Act and enter the Adventure World of the main conflict in the Second Act.
[Write info here]

ACT TWO

(reaction) 25% - 37%
After the First Plot Point, the protagonist scrambles to understand obstacles thrown in his way by the antagonist.
[Write info here]

FIRST PINCH POINT 37% mark
A reminder of the antagonist's power, which provides new clues about the nature of the conflict.
37% The First Pinch Point: Punished for Using Lie
The protagonist is "punished" for using the Lie. In the Normal World, he was able to use the Lie to get the Thing He Wants. But in the Second Act, this is no longer a functional mindset. Throughout the First Half of the Second Act, he will try to use his old Lie-based mindsets to reach his goals and will be "punished" by failures until he begins to learn how things really work.
[Write info here]

(realization) 37% - 50%
Protagonist's realization grows, and his reactions become more informed.
[Write info here]

MIDPOINT 50% mark
The Moment of Truth when the protagonist realizes the central truth about the nature of the conflict.
50% The Midpoint (Second Plot Point): Sees Truth, But Doesn't Yet Reject Lie
The protagonist encounters a Moment of Truth in which he comes face to face with the thematic Truth (often via a simultaneous plot-based revelation about the external conflict). This is the first time the protagonist consciously recognizes the Truth

and its power. He does not yet, however, recognize the Truth and the Lie as incompatible. He will attempt to use both in the Second Half of the Second Act.
[Write info here]

(action) 50% - 62%
Thanks to his new understanding, the protagonist makes headway against antagonist.
[Write info here]

2nd PINCH POINT 62% mark

Foreshadows Third Plot Point and serves to remind the protagonist what is at stake.
62% The Second Pinch Point: Rewarded for Effectively Using Truth
The protagonist is "rewarded" for using the Truth. Building upon what he learned at the Midpoint, the protagonist will start implementing Truth-based actions in combating the antagonistic force and reaching toward the Thing He Wants. He will be "rewarded" by successes as he moves nearer and nearer his ultimate plot goal.
[Write info here]

(renewed push) 62% - 75%
Protagonist renews attack upon antagonist. He reaches a seeming victory.
[Write info here]

ACT THREE

3rd PLOT POINT 75% mark

A dark moment for the character. After the victory at the end of the Second Act, he experiences a reversal.
75% The Third Plot Point: Rejects Lie
The protagonist is confronted by a "low moment" brought about by his continuing refusal to fully reject the Lie. Finally, the protagonist must confront the true stakes of what he stands to lose if he continues to embrace the Lie. Feeling all but defeated, he rejects the Lie. Implicitly, he also fully embraces the Truth.
[Write info here]

(recovery) 75% - 88%

Protagonist reels as he questions his choices, his commitment to his goal, and his own worth and ability.

[Write info here]

CLIMAX BEGINS 88% mark

This turning point forces the protagonist and the antagonist to finally face each other.

88% The Climax: Embraces Truth

The protagonist enters the final confrontation with the antagonistic force to decide whether or not he will gain the Thing He Wants. Directly before or during this section, he consciously and explicitly embraces and wields the Truth.

[Write info here]

(confrontation) 88% - 98%

Duel to the (literal or metaphoric) death. What occurs here ensures protagonist and antagonist cannot both walk away.

[Write info here]

CLIMACTIC MOMENT 98% mark

The moment the protagonist's goal is met, it becomes a physical impossibility for the conflict to continue.

98% The Climactic Moment: Uses Truth to Gain Need

The protagonist uses the Truth and all it has taught him about himself and the conflict to gain the Thing He Needs. Depending upon the nature of his Truth, he may also gain the Thing He Wants, or he may realize he needs to sacrifice it for his own greater good. As a result, he definitively ends the conflict between himself and the antagonistic force.

[Write info here]

(resolution) 98% - 100%

Ease readers out of the excitement of the Climax and into the final emotion.

100% The Resolution: Enters New Truth-Empowered Normal World

The protagonist either enters a new Normal World or returns to the original Normal World, where he can now live as a Truth-empowered individual.

WILLIAM BARTLETT

[Write info here]

EPILOGUE 101%
[Optional]

Thank you and I hope you enjoyed this guide! I sincerely
hope it can help you on your journey to become
a successful and celebrated author!
Please leave me a rating on Amazon! Please leave a review too!
Don't forget to check out my editing services at:
https://www.williambartlettauthor.com/

www.ingramcontent.com/pod-product-compliance
Lightning Source LLC
Chambersburg PA
CBHW040240240726
48664CB00001B/203